Fitbit Charge 5

USER GUIDE

The instructive user manual for Fitbit Charge 5 – hacks, tips & skills and more

Contents

Introduction
Brief overview of Fitbit Charge 5   1
Technical specifications   2

Getting Started
Unboxing and charging the device   4
Installing the Fitbit app on your smartphone   5
Pairing your Fitbit Charge 5 with your smartphone   6
Setting up your Fitbit account   7

Navigating the Device
Understanding the buttons and touch screen interface   9
Accessing menus and apps   10
Customizing your clock face   11

Tracking Your Health and Fitness
Setting fitness goals   13
Using the exercise tracker to track workouts   14
Tracking your heart rate and sleep   15
Setting reminders to move   16

Using the Fitbit App
Syncing your Fitbit Charge 5 with the app   18
Viewing your daily stats   19
Setting up notifications and alerts   20
Connecting with friends and joining challenges   21

Managing Your Device
Adjusting settings and preferences   22
Updating your device software   23
Troubleshooting common issues   24
Replacing the band or charging cable   25

Introduction

Brief overview of Fitbit Charge 5

Welcome to the user guide for the Fitbit Charge 5! The Fitbit Charge 5 is a state-of-the-art fitness tracker designed to help you reach your health and fitness goals. With its sleek design and advanced features, the Charge 5 offers a comprehensive approach to health and wellness, tracking everything from your heart rate and sleep to your daily activity levels and workouts.

This user guide has been created to help you get the most out of your Fitbit Charge 5. Whether you're a fitness enthusiast looking to take your workouts to the next level or simply someone who wants to stay on top of their health, this guide will provide you with all the information you need to use your device effectively.

We'll start by walking you through the setup process, including how to pair your device with your smartphone and set up your Fitbit account. Then, we'll take a closer look at the features and functions of your Fitbit Charge 5, from tracking your heart rate and sleep to setting fitness goals and joining challenges.

We'll also show you how to use the Fitbit app to track your progress and connect with friends, as well as provide tips for managing your device and troubleshooting any issues you may encounter.

By the end of this user guide, you'll be able to use your Fitbit Charge 5 to its fullest potential, empowering you to take control of your health and wellness in a meaningful and sustainable way. So let's get started!

Technical specifications

Here are some technical specifications for the Fitbit Charge 5:

Display:

- 1000 nits bright touchscreen OLED display
- Always-on display mode
- Up to 20 clock faces to choose from

Sensors:

- 3-axis accelerometer
- Optical heart rate sensor
- Skin temperature sensor
- GPS (built-in)

Battery life:

- Up to 7 days (depending on usage)

Water resistance:

- Up to 50 meters
- Wireless connectivity:

- Bluetooth 5.0
- Wi-Fi (802.11 b/g/n)

Compatibility:

- Android and iOS devices (requires Bluetooth and internet connection)

Supported languages:

- English, Spanish, French, German, Italian, Japanese, Dutch, Swedish, Korean, and Portuguese

Dimensions:

- 36.3mm x 28.8mm x 10.5mm

Weight:

- 27g

Materials:

- Watch case made of anodized aluminum
- Back panel made of plastic
- Band made of silicone

Overall, the Fitbit Charge 5 is a well-designed and feature-rich activity tracker that offers advanced health and fitness tracking capabilities, as well as personalized insights and guidance to help users achieve their fitness goals.

Getting Started

Unboxing and charging the device

Unboxing and charging your Fitbit Charge 5 is the first step in using the device. Here are the steps to follow:

1. **Unboxing:** When you first receive your Fitbit Charge 5, open the box and remove the device, charging cable, and any other accessories.
2. **Charging:** To charge your Fitbit Charge 5, connect the charging cable to the device by aligning the pins on the cable with the charging port on the back of the device. The charging cable should snap into place.
3. **Plug in:** Plug the other end of the charging cable into a USB port on your computer or into a USB wall adapter. The device should start charging immediately.
4. **Check battery level:** While charging, the battery icon on your Fitbit Charge 5 will display the current battery level. A full charge can take up to two hours, and the device can last up to 7 days on a single charge.
5. **Disconnect:** Once your Fitbit Charge 5 is fully charged, disconnect the charging cable from the device by gently pulling it out of the charging port.
6. **Turn on:** To turn on your Fitbit Charge 5, press and hold the button on the side of the device until the

Fitbit logo appears. The device should then vibrate and display the time.

By following these steps, you can ensure that your Fitbit Charge 5 is properly charged and ready to use. Remember to charge your device regularly to ensure that it stays powered and ready to track your health and fitness goals.

Installing the Fitbit app on your smartphone

To fully utilize your Fitbit Charge 5, you'll need to install the Fitbit app on your smartphone. Here are the steps to follow:

1. **Compatibility:** First, check that your smartphone is compatible with the Fitbit app. You can check this on the Fitbit website or in your device's app store.
2. **Download:** Next, open your device's app store and search for "Fitbit." Tap on the Fitbit app icon and then tap "Download" or "Get" to start the installation process.
3. **Open app:** Once the app has finished downloading, tap on the app icon to open it.
4. **Create account:** If you don't already have a Fitbit account, you'll need to create one by providing your email address, password, and other basic information. If you already have a Fitbit account, simply log in with your credentials.
5. **Pair device:** Follow the on-screen instructions to pair your Fitbit Charge 5 with the app. This will involve

turning on Bluetooth on your smartphone and bringing the device close to your Fitbit Charge 5.

6. **Sync data:** Once your Fitbit Charge 5 is paired with the app, it will automatically sync data such as your daily activity, heart rate, and sleep information. You can view this information in the app and use it to track your progress towards your health and fitness goals.

By following these steps, you can install the Fitbit app on your smartphone and start using your Fitbit Charge 5 to its fullest potential.

Pairing your Fitbit Charge 5 with your smartphone

Pairing your Fitbit Charge 5 with your smartphone allows you to access additional features and view your health and fitness data on the go. Here are the steps to follow:

1. Turn on Bluetooth: Make sure Bluetooth is turned on for both your smartphone and your Fitbit Charge 5. You can check this by going to the Bluetooth settings on your smartphone and the Settings menu on your Fitbit Charge 5.

2. Open Fitbit app: Open the Fitbit app on your smartphone and tap on the profile icon in the upper left-hand corner of the screen.

3. Tap your device: Tap on "Set up a Device" and select "Fitbit Charge 5" from the list of available devices.
4. Follow instructions: Follow the on-screen instructions to pair your Fitbit Charge 5 with your smartphone. This will involve turning on Bluetooth on your smartphone and bringing the device close to your Fitbit Charge 5.
5. Sync data: Once your Fitbit Charge 5 is paired with your smartphone, it will automatically sync data such as your daily activity, heart rate, and sleep information. You can view this information in the app and use it to track your progress towards your health and fitness goals.

By following these steps, you can pair your Fitbit Charge 5 with your smartphone and start using its full range of features. Keep in mind that you may need to update your Fitbit app or firmware to ensure that everything is working properly.

Setting up your Fitbit account

Setting up a Fitbit account is necessary to fully utilize your Fitbit Charge 5 and track your health and fitness progress. Here are the steps to follow:

1. Download the Fitbit app: Download the Fitbit app on your smartphone from the App Store or Google Play.

2. Open the app: Once the app is downloaded, open it on your smartphone.

3. Sign up or log in: If you don't have a Fitbit account, tap "Join Fitbit" and follow the on-screen instructions to create an account. If you already have a Fitbit account, tap "Log In" and enter your credentials.

4. Enter your information: Once you're signed in, you'll be prompted to enter your personal information, such as your height, weight, and age. This information helps Fitbit calculate your daily activity and health goals.

5. Sync your device: Follow the on-screen instructions to sync your Fitbit Charge 5 with the Fitbit app. This will allow your device to automatically track and log your daily activity and health data.

6. Customize your settings: You can customize your device settings and app preferences in the Fitbit app, such as your goal progress, notifications, and reminders.

By following these steps, you can set up your Fitbit account and start tracking your health and fitness progress with your Fitbit Charge 5. Remember to keep your account information up-to-date and synced with your device for accurate tracking.

Navigating Fitbit Charge 5

Understanding the buttons and touch screen interface

Understanding the buttons and touch screen interface of your Fitbit Charge 5 is essential for navigating the device and accessing its features. Here's a breakdown of the buttons and touch screen interface:

- **Button:** Your Fitbit Charge 5 has a single button on the left side of the device. Pressing this button will wake up the screen, take you back to the previous screen, or confirm a selection.
- **Touch screen:** The touch screen on your Fitbit Charge 5 allows you to swipe and tap to access different features and menus. You can swipe up or down to view different menus or settings, swipe left or right to view different screens, and tap on icons or options to select them.
- **Quick Access:** The touch screen also has a Quick Access feature that allows you to customize the screen with up to six of your favorite apps or features. You can access these by swiping left from the home screen or pressing and holding the button.
- **Always-On Display:** The Fitbit Charge 5 also has an Always-On Display feature that keeps the time and important information visible at all times. To enable or

disable this feature, go to the settings menu in the Fitbit app.

By familiarizing yourself with the buttons and touch screen interface of your Fitbit Charge 5, you can easily navigate the device and access its features.

Accessing menus and apps

Accessing menus and apps on your Fitbit Charge 5 allows you to view and manage your health and fitness data, set goals, and access other features. Here's how to access menus and apps on your device:

- **Wake up the screen:** To access menus and apps, you'll need to wake up the screen on your Fitbit Charge 5. You can do this by pressing the button on the left side of the device or by tapping the screen.
- **Swipe up or down:** To access different menus or settings, swipe up or down on the touch screen. You can swipe up to view your stats, swipe down to access notifications or settings, or swipe left or right to view other screens.
- **Tap on icons:** To select a menu or app, tap on the corresponding icon on the screen. For example, you can tap on the Exercise app to start a workout, or tap on the Sleep app to view your sleep data.
- **Use Quick Access:** If you've set up Quick Access, you can access your favorite apps or features by swiping

left from the home screen or pressing and holding the button.

- **Customize settings:** You can customize your device settings and preferences by accessing the settings menu in the Fitbit app. This allows you to change things like your goal progress, notifications, and reminders.

By accessing menus and apps on your Fitbit Charge 5, you can view your health and fitness data, manage your goals, and access other features.

Customizing your clock face

Customizing your clock face on your Fitbit Charge 5 allows you to personalize your device and view the information that's most important to you. Here's how to customize your clock face:

1. Wake up the screen: To customize your clock face, you'll need to wake up the screen on your Fitbit Charge 5. You can do this by pressing the button on the left side of the device or by tapping the screen.
2. Swipe up or down: Swipe up or down on the touch screen to access the clock face menu.
3. Tap on "Clock Faces": Tap on "Clock Faces" to view the available clock faces.
4. Choose a clock face: Browse through the available clock faces and select the one that you want to use.

5. Customize the clock face: Once you've selected a clock face, you may have the option to customize it. This can include changing the color, layout, and information displayed on the clock face. Follow the on-screen instructions to customize the clock face to your liking.
6. Save the changes: Once you've customized your clock face, be sure to save your changes before exiting the menu.

By customizing your clock face on your Fitbit Charge 5, you can personalize your device and view the information that's most important to you. If you're unsure how to customize your clock face, consult the user guide or reach out to Fitbit support.

Tracking Your Health and Fitness

Setting fitness goals

Setting fitness goals on your Fitbit Charge 5 allows you to track your progress and stay motivated as you work towards your desired fitness level. Here's how to set fitness goals on your device:

1. Wake up the screen: To set fitness goals on your Fitbit Charge 5, you'll need to wake up the screen. You can do this by pressing the button on the left side of the device or by tapping the screen.
2. Swipe up or down: Swipe up or down on the touch screen to access the "Goals" menu.
3. Tap on "Goals": Tap on "Goals" to access the goals menu.
4. Choose a goal: Select the type of goal you want to set. This could include steps, distance, calories, active minutes, or other metrics.
5. Set a target: Set a target for your goal by entering the desired number of steps, distance, calories, or active minutes you want to achieve.
6. Customize the goal: You can also customize your goal by setting the time frame for achieving it, choosing a different type of goal, or adjusting the target number as needed.

7. Save the goal: Once you've set your goal, be sure to save it before exiting the menu.

By setting fitness goals on your Fitbit Charge 5, you can track your progress and stay motivated as you work towards your desired fitness level.

Using the exercise tracker to track workouts

The exercise tracker on your Fitbit Charge 5 allows you to track your workouts and monitor your progress towards your fitness goals. Here's how to use the exercise tracker on your device:

Wake up the screen: To use the exercise tracker on your Fitbit Charge 5, you'll need to wake up the screen. You can do this by pressing the button on the left side of the device or by tapping the screen.

1. Swipe left: Swipe left on the touch screen to access the Exercise app.
2. Choose an exercise: Select the type of exercise you want to track by tapping on the corresponding icon. You can choose from activities such as running, biking, swimming, and more.
3. Start the workout: Once you've selected the exercise, tap on the "Start" button to begin the workout.
4. Monitor progress: During the workout, you can monitor your progress by viewing data such as

distance, time, heart rate, and calories burned on the screen.

5. End the workout: When you're finished with the workout, tap on the "Finish" button to end the session and save your data.

6. Review workout data: After the workout is finished, you can review your data in the Exercise app or in the Fitbit app on your smartphone.

By using the exercise tracker on your Fitbit Charge 5, you can track your workouts and monitor your progress towards your fitness goals. If you're unsure how to use the exercise tracker on your device, consult the user guide or reach out to Fitbit support.

Tracking your heart rate and sleep

Your Fitbit Charge 5 tracks your heart rate and sleep to help you monitor your health and fitness levels. Here's how to track your heart rate and sleep on your device:

1. **Heart rate tracking:** Your Fitbit Charge 5 continuously tracks your heart rate throughout the day and during workouts. To view your heart rate data, simply wake up the screen and swipe up or down to access the "Heart Rate" menu. You can view your current heart rate, resting heart rate, and heart rate trends over time.

2. **Sleep tracking:** Your Fitbit Charge 5 also tracks your sleep patterns to help you monitor the quality and duration of your sleep. To track your sleep, wear your device to bed and it will automatically detect when you fall asleep and wake up. In the morning, wake up the screen and swipe up or down to access the "Sleep" menu. You can view data such as your time asleep, time awake, and sleep stages.
3. **Sync your data:** To ensure that your heart rate and sleep data is accurate and up-to-date, be sure to sync your device regularly with the Fitbit app on your smartphone.

By tracking your heart rate and sleep on your Fitbit Charge 5, you can monitor your health and fitness levels and make adjustments to your lifestyle as needed.

Setting reminders to move

Setting reminders to move on your Fitbit Charge 5 can help you maintain an active lifestyle throughout the day. Here's how to set reminders to move on your device:

1. Wake up the screen: To set reminders to move on your Fitbit Charge 5, you'll need to wake up the screen. You can do this by pressing the button on the left side of the device or by tapping the screen.
2. Swipe up or down: Swipe up or down on the touch screen to access the "Reminders to Move" menu.

3. Tap on "Reminders to Move": Tap on "Reminders to Move" to access the menu.
4. Set a reminder: Select the frequency at which you want to receive reminders to move, such as every hour or every 30 minutes. You can also customize the time range during which you want to receive reminders.
5. Save the reminder: Once you've set your reminder, be sure to save it before exiting the menu.

By setting reminders to move on your Fitbit Charge 5, you can maintain an active lifestyle throughout the day and improve your overall health and fitness levels.

Using the Fitbit App

Syncing your Fitbit Charge 5 with the app

Syncing your Fitbit Charge 5 with the Fitbit app on your smartphone is important to ensure that your device has the most up-to-date data and to access additional features. Here's how to sync your Fitbit Charge 5 with the app:

1. Open the Fitbit app: Open the Fitbit app on your smartphone.
2. Make sure Bluetooth is on: Make sure that Bluetooth is enabled on your smartphone.
3. Tap on your profile picture: Tap on your profile picture in the top left corner of the app.
4. Tap on your device: Tap on your Fitbit Charge 5 in the list of connected devices.
5. Tap on "Sync Now": Tap on "Sync Now" to initiate the sync process.
6. Wait for the sync to complete: Wait for the sync to complete, which may take a few minutes depending on the amount of data that needs to be transferred.
7. Review your data: After the sync is complete, you can review your data in the Fitbit app and view your progress towards your fitness goals.

By syncing your Fitbit Charge 5 with the Fitbit app on your smartphone, you can ensure that your device has the most up-to-date data and access additional features such as personalized insights and challenges.

Viewing your daily stats

Viewing your daily stats on your Fitbit Charge 5 can help you monitor your progress towards your fitness goals and make adjustments to your lifestyle as needed. Here's how to view your daily stats on your device:

1. Wake up the screen: To view your daily stats on your Fitbit Charge 5, you'll need to wake up the screen. You can do this by pressing the button on the left side of the device or by tapping the screen.
2. Swipe up or down: Swipe up or down on the touch screen to access the "Today" menu.
3. View your stats: In the "Today" menu, you can view your daily stats such as your steps taken, distance traveled, calories burned, active minutes, heart rate, and more.
4. Access additional menus: To access additional menus and features, such as tracking your exercise or viewing your sleep data, swipe left or right on the touch screen.

By viewing your daily stats on your Fitbit Charge 5, you can monitor your progress towards your fitness goals and make adjustments to your lifestyle as needed.

Setting up notifications and alerts

Setting up notifications and alerts on your Fitbit Charge 5 can help you stay connected and informed throughout the day without having to constantly check your smartphone. Here's how to set up notifications and alerts on your device:

1. Open the Fitbit app: Open the Fitbit app on your smartphone.
2. Tap on your profile picture: Tap on your profile picture in the top left corner of the app.
3. Tap on your device: Tap on your Fitbit Charge 5 in the list of connected devices.
4. Tap on "Notifications": Tap on "Notifications" to access the menu.
5. Customize your notifications: Customize the notifications that you want to receive on your device, such as incoming calls, texts, and app notifications. You can also customize the vibration patterns and enable do not disturb mode.
6. Save your settings: Once you've customized your notifications, be sure to save your settings before exiting the menu.

By setting up notifications and alerts on your Fitbit Charge 5, you can stay connected and informed throughout the day without having to constantly check your smartphone. If you're unsure how to set up notifications and alerts on your device, consult the user guide or reach out to Fitbit support.

Connecting with friends and joining challenges

Connecting with friends and joining challenges on your Fitbit Charge 5 can help you stay motivated and reach your fitness goals by competing with others and sharing your progress. Here's how to connect with friends and join challenges on your device:

1. Open the Fitbit app: Open the Fitbit app on your smartphone.
2. Tap on the "Community" tab: Tap on the "Community" tab in the bottom navigation bar of the app.
3. Add friends: To connect with friends, tap on the "Add Friends" button and search for their username or email address. You can also connect with Facebook friends who use Fitbit.
4. Join challenges: To join a challenge, tap on the "Challenges" tab and browse the available challenges. You can join challenges such as step challenges, distance challenges, and active minutes challenges.
5. Create challenges: If you want to create your own challenge, tap on the "Create Challenge" button and customize the challenge parameters.
6. Track your progress: Once you've joined a challenge or connected with friends, you can track your progress and view your ranking in the challenge leaderboard.

Managing your Device

Adjusting settings and preferences

Adjusting settings and preferences on your Fitbit Charge 5 can help you customize your device to your personal preferences and optimize its functionality. Here's how to adjust settings and preferences on your device:

1. Open the Fitbit app: Open the Fitbit app on your smartphone.
2. Tap on your profile picture: Tap on your profile picture in the top left corner of the app.
3. Tap on your device: Tap on your Fitbit Charge 5 in the list of connected devices.
4. Customize your settings: Customize the settings and preferences that you want to adjust, such as language, time format, unit of measurement, and more. You can also adjust settings for notifications, alarms, and other features.
5. Save your settings: Once you've adjusted your settings, be sure to save your changes before exiting the menu.

By adjusting settings and preferences on your Fitbit Charge 5, you can customize your device to your personal preferences and optimize its functionality.

Updating your device software

Updating your device software on your Fitbit Charge 5 can help ensure that your device is running smoothly and has the latest features and improvements. Here's how to update your device software:

1. Connect to Wi-Fi: Make sure that your Fitbit Charge 5 is connected to Wi-Fi.
2. Open the Fitbit app: Open the Fitbit app on your smartphone.
3. Tap on your profile picture: Tap on your profile picture in the top left corner of the app.
4. Tap on your device: Tap on your Fitbit Charge 5 in the list of connected devices.
5. Tap on "About": Tap on "About" to access the device information menu.
6. Check for updates: Check for updates by tapping on "Check for device update". If an update is available, follow the prompts to download and install the update.
7. Wait for the update to complete: Once the update has been downloaded, your device will restart and the update will install. This may take several minutes, so be patient and wait for the process to complete.

By updating your device software on your Fitbit Charge 5, you can ensure that your device is running smoothly and has the latest features and improvements.

Troubleshooting common issues

If you experience issues with your Fitbit Charge 5, there are a few troubleshooting steps you can take to resolve common issues. Here are some common issues and troubleshooting steps:

1. **Device not syncing:** If your device is not syncing with the Fitbit app, try the following:
   - Make sure your device is within range of your smartphone.
   - Ensure that Bluetooth is turned on and the Fitbit app is allowed to access it.
   - Restart your device and the Fitbit app.
   - Try turning Bluetooth off and on again.
2. **Battery life issues:** If you're experiencing battery life issues, try the following:
   - Make sure that you're using the original charger and that it's connected properly.
   - Restart your device.
   - Reduce the frequency of use of certain features like GPS, music playback, or notifications.
   - Turn off always-on display if you're not using it.
3. **Heart rate monitor issues:** If you're having trouble with your heart rate monitor, try the following:
   - Make sure your device is in contact with your skin.
   - Check that the band is fitted correctly and not too loose.

- Make sure the heart rate sensor is clean and free of debris.
4. **Display issues:** If you're experiencing issues with your display, try the following:
    - Clean the screen with a soft, dry cloth.
    - Try adjusting the brightness of the screen in settings.
    - Restart your device.

Replacing the band or charging cable

If you need to replace the band or charging cable for your Fitbit Charge 5, here are the steps to follow:

Replacing the band:

5. Purchase a replacement band: You can purchase replacement bands from Fitbit or from third-party retailers.
6. Remove the old band: Press the button on the back of your device and slide the band off.
7. Attach the new band: Align the pins on the new band with the slots on your device and slide it into place until it clicks.

Replacing the charging cable:

1. Purchase a replacement cable: You can purchase replacement charging cables from Fitbit or from third-party retailers.

2. Remove the old cable: Gently pull the charging cable out of the back of your device.
3. Insert the new cable: Insert the new charging cable into the back of your device and make sure it clicks into place.

Note: When replacing the band or charging cable, be sure to use only Fitbit-approved accessories to avoid damaging your device.

With these simple steps, you can easily replace the band or charging cable for your Fitbit Charge 5..

Printed in Great Britain
by Amazon